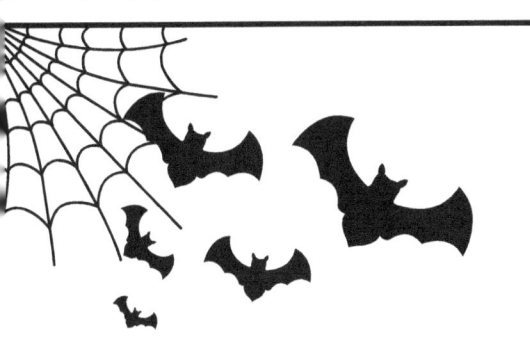

This Book Belongs to

_____

_____

_____

Copyright © 2019
by Kolme Korkeudet Oy
🎃 All Rights Reserved 🎃

No part
of this book may be
reproduced in any form
or by any electronic or
mechanical means, including
information storage and
retrieval systems, without
written permission from the
author, except for the use of
brief quotations in
a book review.

Draw the Picture
Step by Step

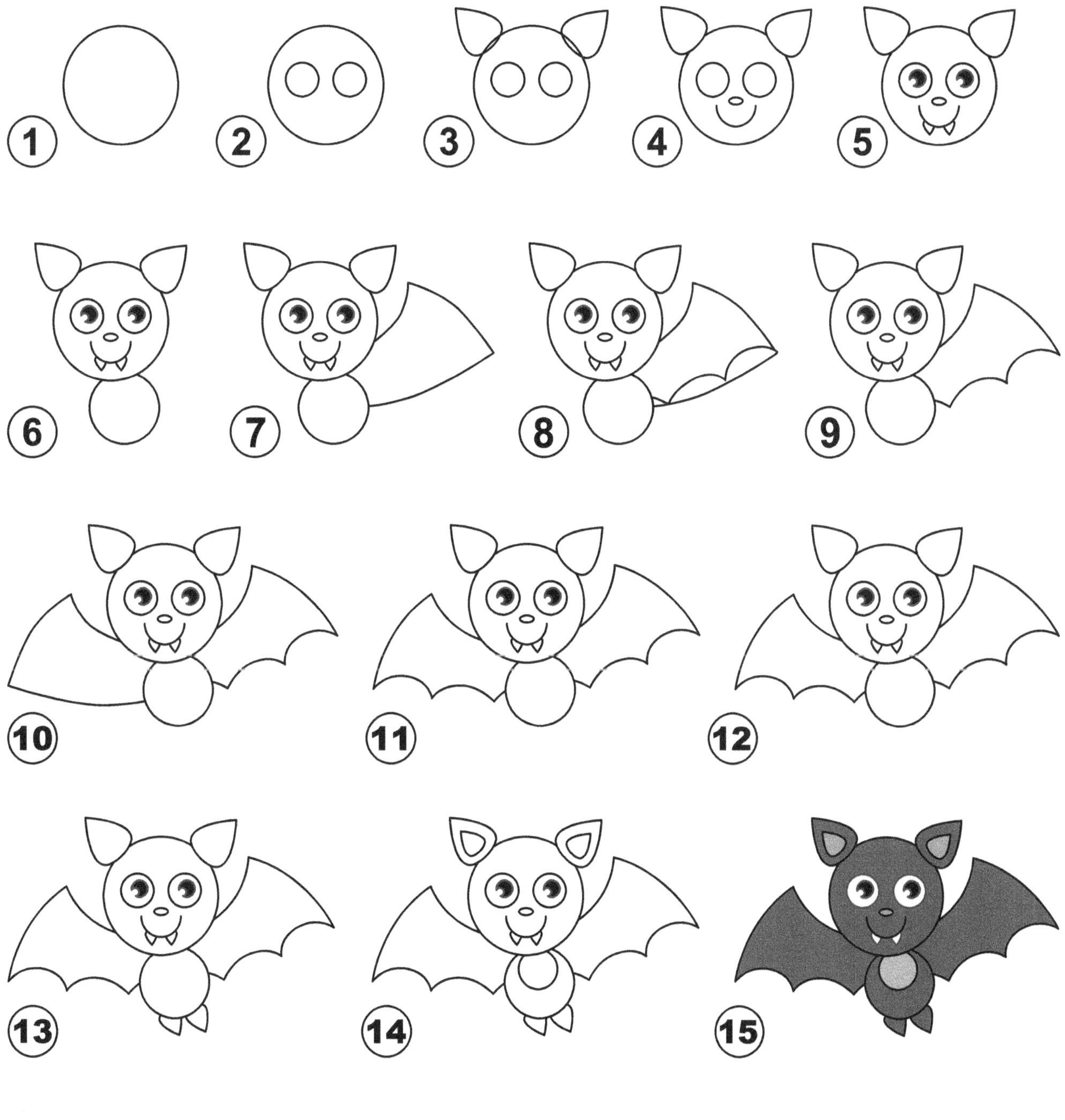

Connect the Dots

COLOR THE PICTURE

FIND THE CORRECT SHADOW

1

2

3

4

SEARCH THE WORD
SOLVE THE REBUS

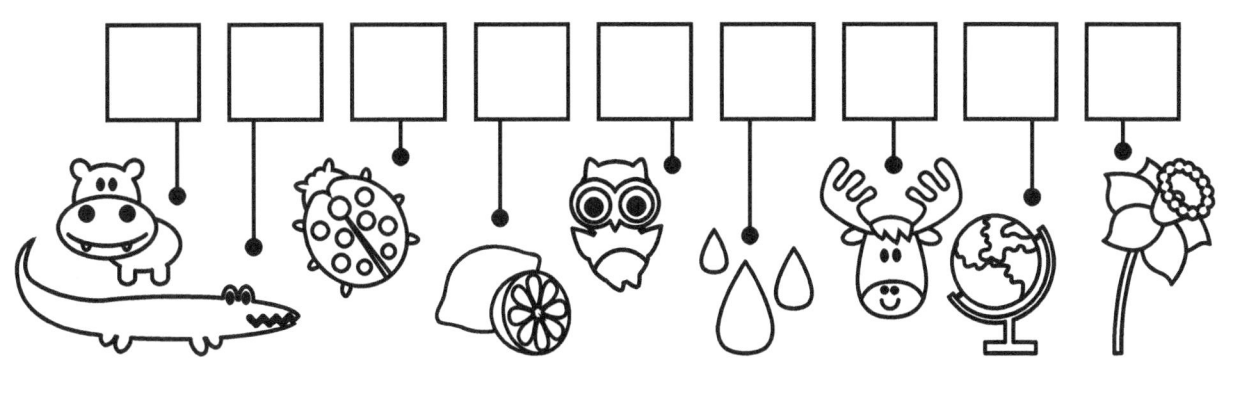

COPY THE PICTURE
USING THE GRID

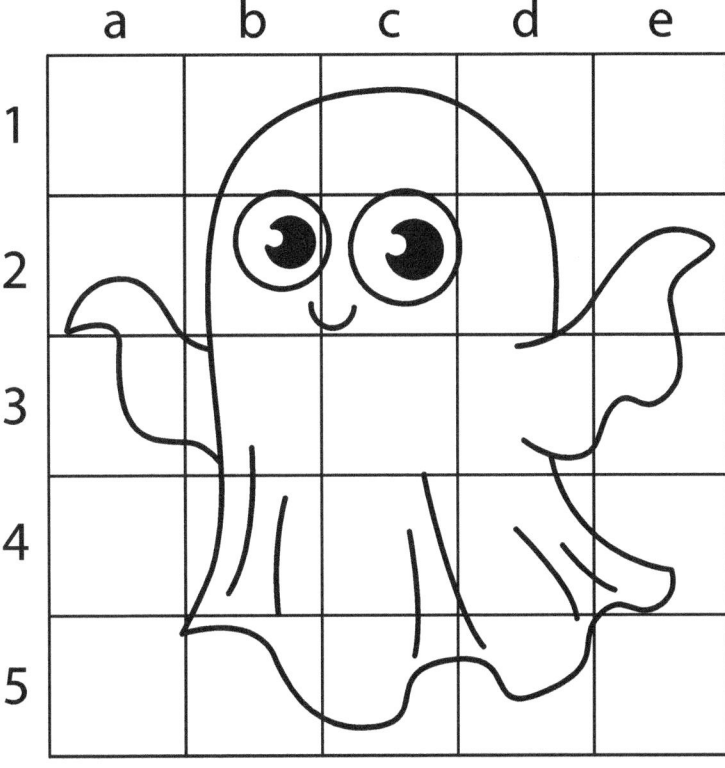

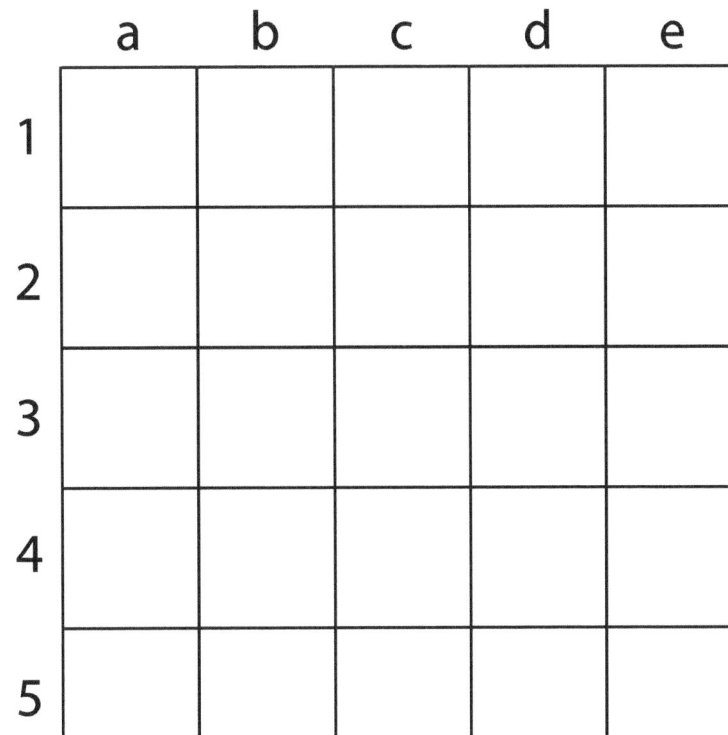

MAZE GAME

COLOR THE PICTURE

Connect the Dots

DRAW THE PICTURE
STEP BY STEP

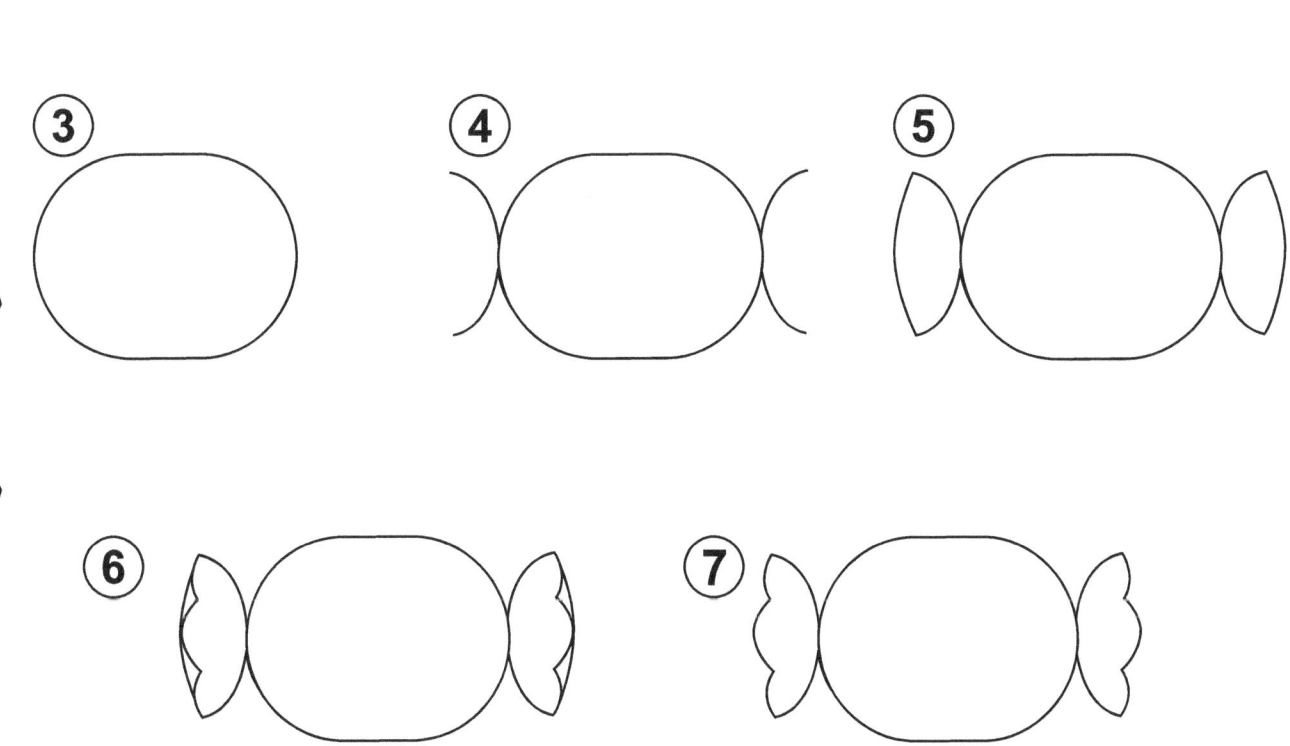
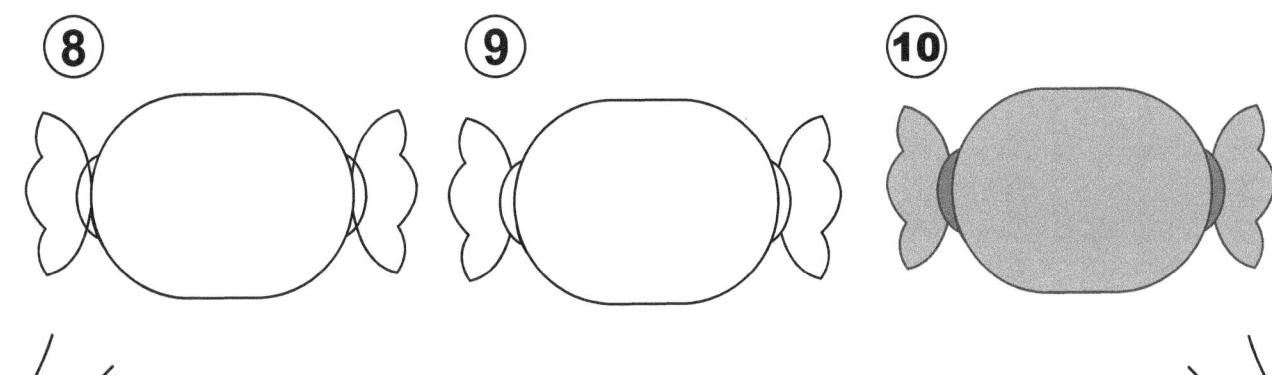

WORDS GAME

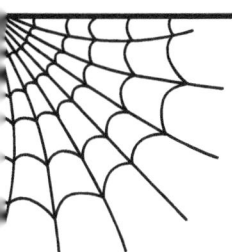
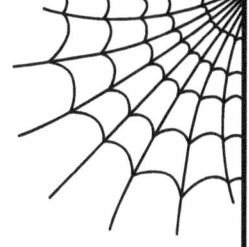

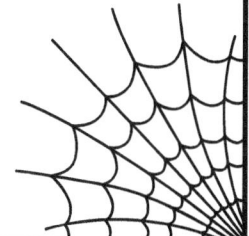

D	P	G	R
C	A	N	W
U	N	O	F
K	D	Y	L

K	U	A	U
S	P	K	J
H	M	I	N
P	U	P	F

Y	G	F	K
B	H	O	M
G	D	S	V
N	B	T	Z

C	A	V	H
K	N	D	Y
T	J	L	G
A	O	E	H

COLOR THE PICTURE

Copy the Picture
Using the Grid

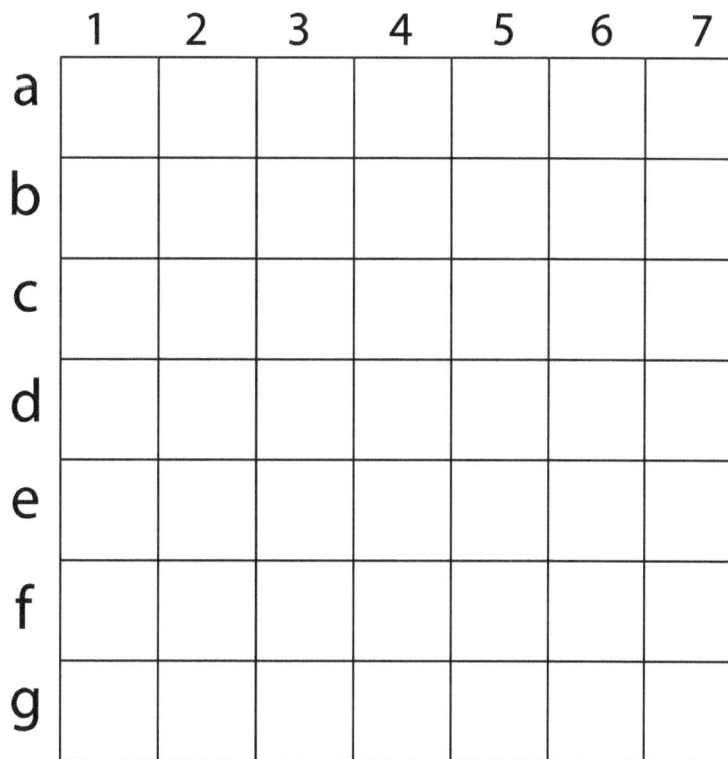

Find Letters V
Color the Space Dark Grey

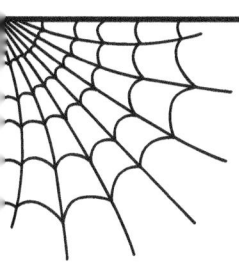

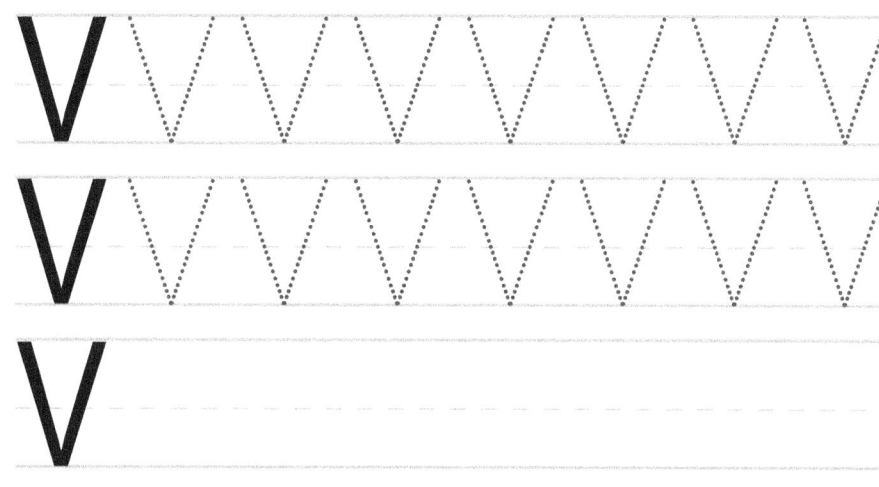

MAZE GAME

COLOR THE PICTURE

COMPLETE THE PICTURE

MAZE GAME

WORDS GAME

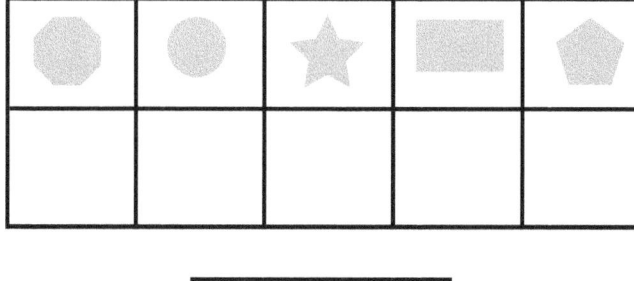

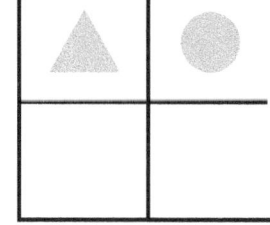

MAZE GAME

ANSWERS

HALLOWEEN

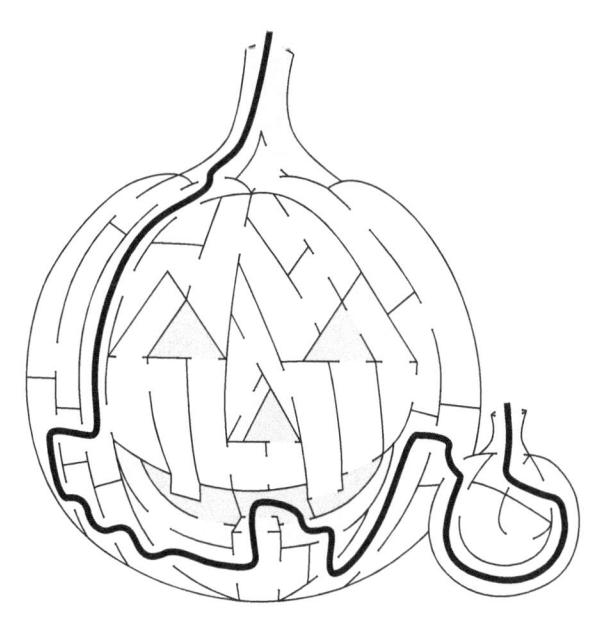

ANSWERS

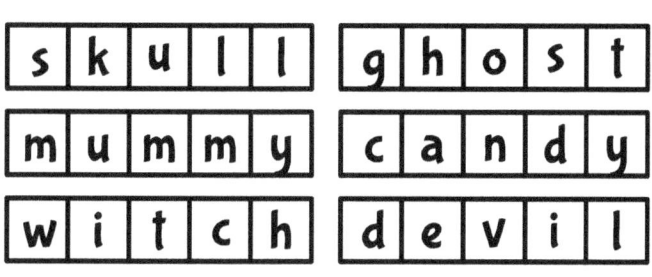

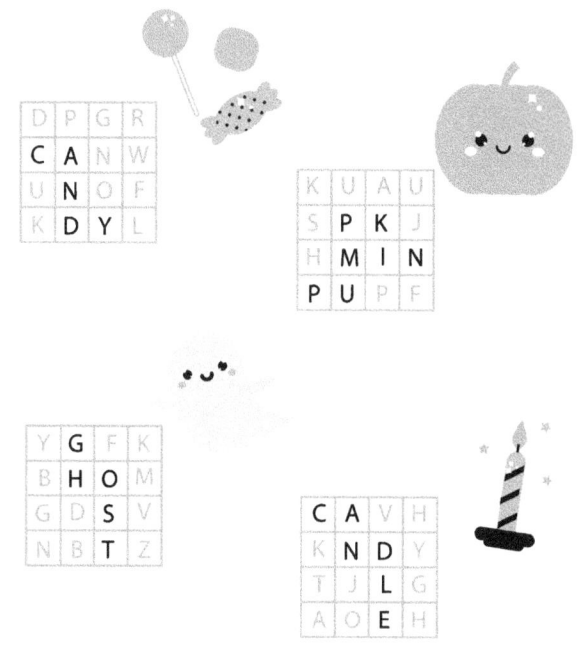

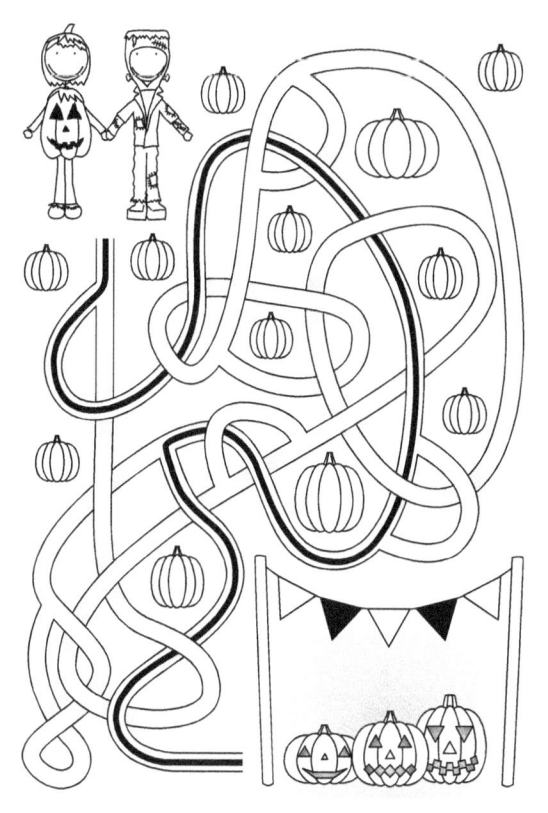

ANSWERS

TRICK

OR

TREAT

ANSWERS

www.ingramcontent.com/pod-product-compliance
Lightning Source LLC
Chambersburg PA
CBHW081510080526
44589CB00017B/2712